How to Change Your Financial Trajectory

Written by David Saucer

Critical Praise for
The CA$H Residence

"In *"The CA$H Residence"*, author David Saucer crystallizes the complex and makes it incredibly simple. He dishes out an understanding of PES (Personalized Economic System) like a gourmet chef serves a fine meal; only Saucer gives you the whole satisfying taste in what seems like one savory bite…Saucer makes the American Dream seem doable and achievable even on a limited household income. He removes the confusion and the sense of overwhelming and replaces it with financial hope. Consistency, long-term commitment, and a simple strategy equate to a debt free and prosperous life with you in the driver's seat…As one who has purchased countless books that cost me money but never provided a return on my investment, I delight in discovering this goldmine in print that opens an immediate pathway to lifetime financial freedom."

>Dr. Fred Childs, Executive Coach, Mentor, Author, Entrepreneur, and Minister

"In my opinion, the book you currently hold in your hand is one of the most concise and relevant in the market today… David Saucer has over two decades of experience in the financial services industry. His ability to communicate

intricate financial ideas in a simple manner will make this book a very valuable resource."
> B. Chase Chandler, Best-Selling Author of *The Wealthy Physician* and *The Wealthy Family*

"I have read David's book cover to cover, and I believe that it will help anyone who is looking to be more efficient with their dollars. Creating long term wealth is not about a particular investment vehicle, but about **process**. David does a great job of explaining the process of how we should all think about our money, and also explains the instrument that can be used to warehouse the dollars until a great opportunity presents itself."
> Jay Gentry (Financial Services Industry Veteran)

"David has taken the complex and made it accessible! This book is carefully crafted and filled with meaningful examples. A user-friendly read."
> Dr. Robert Hogan, Assistant Professor of Accounting

The Cash Residence: How to Change Your Financial Trajectory

Copyright © 2014 by (David Saucer)

All rights reserved. No part of this book may be reproduced or transmitted in any form or by any means without written permission from the author.

Disclaimer: This book is meant to provide general information on financial subjects and strategies. It should not be used as sole guidance for making financial decisions. Mr. Saucer recommends that you seek a qualified and experienced professional when implementing a financial strategy or purchasing any investment or insurance product. The author assumes no responsibility for any errors or omissions.

The contents of this book are the opinions of Mr. David Saucer at the time of this writing. For educational use only.

Printed in USA

David Saucer

To my girl, Cindy and our children, Kaleb and Chloe'.
Thank you for following me when I chose the "The Road not Taken."

**Two roads diverged in a wood, and I —
I took the one less traveled by,
and that has made all the difference.
~ Robert Frost**

Contents

DEDICATION..............................…..…5

FORWARD..............................……..10
B. Chase Chandler

PREFACE..............................……..12

INTRODUCTION..........................14
What Color is the Ambulance?

PART ONE
CHAPTER 1: An Objective Look at Financial Decisions..17
What's the best way to decide your financial future?

CHAPTER 2: Conventional Wisdom is an Oxymoron..21
Following the herd isn't always the best choice.

CHAPTER 3: The Herd Effect..…...23
Collective behavior happens in instructive ways.

CHAPTER 4: The Parable of the Ham...…......24
Conventional wisdom, or accident?

CHAPTER 5: Stress, Uncertainty, and the
Future..27
Procrastination comes with a cost.

PART TWO
CHAPTER 6: 3 Types of
People...31
Introducing the CA$H Residence Concept.

CHAPTER 7: Taxes – Up or
Down?..34
Exploring the effect of taxes on financial planning.

CHAPTER 8: The Perfect
Asset?..40
What's the best vehicle for your investment dollars?

CHAPTER 9: 401k
Chaos...43
Learn why the 401k isn't always the best retirement choice.

PART THREE
CHAPTER 10: What do Banks
Know?..46
Where do banks and corporations put their money to make it grow?

CHAPTER 11: The Phenomenon of Uninterrupted Compound Interest..50
What is the Bible's position on wealth creation?

CHAPTER 12: Famous Examples of CA$H Residence or PES Phenomenon...54
Famous names, unusual stories.

CHAPTER 13: Public Company or Mutual Company?..60
Why do they treat their clients differently?

Chapter 14: CA$H Residence—a Personalized Economic System..62
Learn the benefits of the CA$H Residence approach.

CHAPTER 15: CA$H Residence for Business...64
Business owners can benefit from the same approach.

CHAPTER 16: Case Studies..66
How does a personalized economic system look in action?

EPILOGUE: The Journey to Freedom..69

ABOUT THE AUTHOR..71

Appendix A: Types of Life Insurance..72
Appendix B: A Personal Plan for Financial Success...73
Appendix C: Suggested Reading..76

Citations..77

Forward by B. Chase Chandler

In my opinion, the book you currently hold in your hand is one of the most concise and relevant in the market today. Giving this reading your full and undivided attention could be the most impactful financial decision you make this year. David Saucer has over two decades of experience in the financial services industry. His ability to communicate intricate financial ideas in a simple manner will make this book a very valuable resource.

The strategies and principles David delineates, while somewhat unknown to the majority, are those that have helped some of the most successful people in our country's success build their businesses. As you read, I think you'll find that the unconventional thoughts shared will begin to excite you as you see the vision of what's possible.

Unfortunately, there are many who will disregard or refuse to study what Mr. Saucer is giving. Many financial 'gurus', family members, friends, and colleagues will not understand how important these issues are. As you will soon appreciate, it is vital to keep an objective point of view while internalizing this material.

David Saucer

I can tell you one thing for sure—these ideas have changed my life. Yes, there are some who still do not understand, some individuals that I am (or was) very close to. Even so, the truth will set you free. Let the truth set *you* free.

B. Chase Chandler
Best-Selling Author of
The Wealthy Physician and *The Wealthy Family*

Preface

I have friends and clients whose chosen career path was working a job with the state government or a municipality, and they longed for the day retirement would come. They worked specifically for the future and for the pension they would receive. But as with most entrepreneurs or business owners, if there was to be a retirement plan or a pension, it would be up to them to prepare for it individually.

I've always looked for the most efficient financial vehicle to lead my family to personal financial freedom and designing a predictable retirement (should we ever choose to retire).

My search has taken me all over the country; attending workshops, seminars, and reading hundreds of books. Long hours of study refined my understanding of the subject of financial freedom.

What I found was a 200-year-old method, not the likely path for most. Quite honestly, the method fit my personality or the factors in my DNA. Choosing the road not taken, the path the crowds did not travel, the solution outside the box always appealed to me.

And the method works. Every day brings me a better understanding (and more commitment to) this unusual method.

Let me warn you, though. If you're a pesimist, if you're close-minded, or you are the kind of person who craves the validation of the masses, this method won't be for you. And I can pass a kind of savings on to you now: Don't read on.

David A. Saucer

Introduction: What Color is the Ambulance?

Here's an interesting thought I encountered recently. I'm going to tell you a story, and then I'm going to ask you a question:

Mr. John Everybody is eating a steak at a nice restaurant. He's relaxed, and he's feeling pretty good. Then something happens. His arm goes numb and he feels sharp chest pains. He knows the signs, and he's smart enough to ask the waitress for help. The restaurant staff is frantic to find help. The manager calls 911, and very soon, the emergency vehicle arrives. The trained paramedics begin to check John's vitals while assessing the current situation. In a moment, the decision is made to rush John to the closest hospital. As the vehicle races through the streets, the paramedics tend to their patient. John arrives, and the properly trained nurses and doctors are there waiting. Thanks to the quick action of professionals, John is going to be okay.

And now, let me ask you a question: What color is the ambulance? Such an odd question for a person who is in need of help, right? I would assume John's answer would be, "Really? I don't remember what color the ambulance was and I don't care. My only concern was arriving where I needed to go, and to get the help I needed to get."

To the person in need, it would not matter if the rescue vehicle was a:
- Red Pickup
- Blue Dump truck
- Horse and Buggy (Okay, a *fast* horse and buggy!)

This book is designed to share information which could change the trajectory of a person's financial future. In today's precarious financial environment, an "ambulance" would be welcome to some. But what if—strapped to the gurney—John Everybody had cried, "Wait just a minute! Are you kidding me? A lime green ambulance? No way! I'm staying here!" What if he *did* care that the ambulance wasn't the standard color emergency vehicle? What if he expected the red-and-white van that everyone else gets in an emergency?

After all, if one particular financial solution was perfect for a large number of people, then most everybody would already be on board, right?

Unless, of course, there was a reason that Wall Street and financial advisors steered clear of a particular solution. If, for example, those advisors forfeited 50-75 percent of their normal fee in recommending this particular option to the client.

But before we go any further, let's define some terms. Read on!

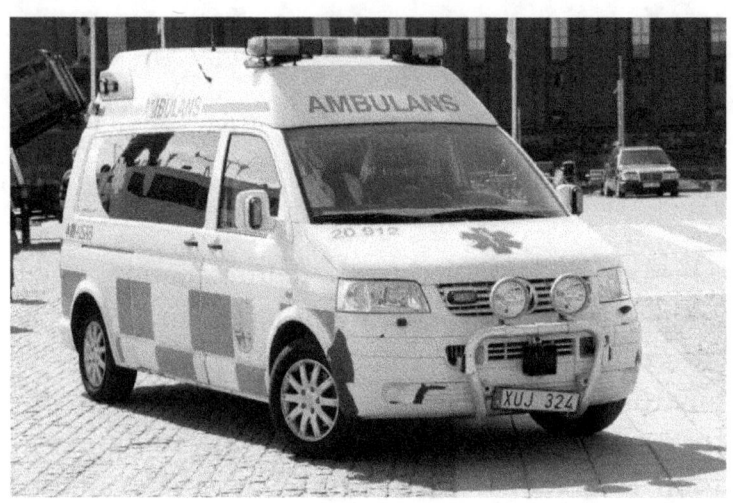

Part One
Chapter 1: An Objective Look at Financial Decisions

This short chapter is going to talk about what guides financial decisions. Along the way, we'll mention a few useful terms that will come up as we explore various financial strategies.

First, some definitions:
- A **Subjective** decision will include feelings and emotions.
- An **Objective** decision will be based on historical data and hard facts. Though feelings are important, when it comes to money, decisions should have a factual basis. That's why, throughout the course of this book, we'll rely heavily on the objective viewpoint.
- **Uninterrupted Compound Interest** is an amazing phenomenon that I'll refer to as the "Eighth Wonder of the World. You'll see why later on in the book.
- **Financial Vehicle** is a term referring to a place to hold money and/or produce some sort of return. Shares of stock are a financial vehicle. So is a savings account. We use the metaphor of a *vehicle* because the purpose of a

financial vehicle is to "get somewhere"—somewhere nice like a comfortable retirement.

The purpose of this book is to suggest a time-honored but out-of-the-ordinary financial vehicle. And the vehicle metaphor is even more useful when you make a direct comparison between cars and financial choices.

When you make a car purchase, what are the things you consider before buying? Depending on who you are, the list might vary. For example, a young couple with an infant might rank safety pretty high on the list. A successful businessman may want a prestigious car. What *options* do you find important in a car?

- Safety
- Speed
- Handling
- A Track Record of Performance
- Low Operating Cost
- Efficiency

Everything in life is somewhere else, and you get there in a car.

~E. B. White

Likewise, we choose our financial vehicles with a list of options. And in many cases, the criteria are the same as those for your car:

- Safety - You don't want to lose your money overnight!
- Speed - How fast will your investment grow?
- Handling - You want control and use of your funds.
- A Track Record of Performance - Not a recent gimmick.
- Low Operating Cost – You want your financial vehicle to make money for you, not your financial advisor.
- Efficiency – You want advantageous tax treatment.

Every automobile has basic parts (such as an engine, tires and the frame). But the cost and value of each vehicle is also determined by the options or amenities the vehicle carries. Cloth or leather seats? Sound system? Tinted windows?

Over the course of this book, I will compare the most common financial vehicles and the features and benefits included in each one. We choose our financial vehicles in the same way we choose our automobiles. Most likely, we compare the options and features and make an educated decision based on an objective view.

Of course, some people make their choices for *subjective* reasons. A car looks cool, so it must be safe, right? The neighbors bought the same model as the man down the street. That means the car has low operating costs, right?

As you read, keep these criteria in mind. Do you want a fast, safe financial vehicle with a proven track record for success and durability? Read on.

Chapter 2: Conventional Wisdom is an Oxymoron

Conventional Wisdom is the body of ideas that's accepted as truth by the public. *Conventional* means generally accepted. Orthodox. (Unoriginal.) *Wisdom* is a scholarly body of knowledge. Now here's a thought: Conventional thought is generally accepted without close objective examination. And wisdom is scholarly thought, examined closely and revised as new knowledge becomes available.

Doesn't it strike you that conventional, unexamined thought can't also be considered wisdom? That means "conventional wisdom" is an oxymoron—an inherently contradictory term, like *jumbo shrimp* and *heavy diet*.

The fact is, the progress of mankind can be marked by the mistaken notions of conventional wisdom, from the belief in a "flat earth" to the belief that the "stock market is safe." Nuggets of so-called conventional wisdom are not only unexamined, they are often dead wrong.

- In 1899, Charles Duell, an official at the U.S. Patent Office, noted, *"Everything that can be invented has been invented."* Two years

later, vacuum cleaners were invented. The year after that, air-conditioning.
- Lord Kelvin, President of the Royal Society, echoed popular sentiment when he said, "X-rays will prove to be a hoax."
- Thomas Watson, President of the Board at IBM, said, "I think there's a world market for maybe five computers."

Worse, conventional wisdom is often an obstacle to the acceptance of newly acquired information, to introducing new theories and explanations. "Wisdom" acts as a barrier that must be overcome by legitimate alternative views.

Will conventional wisdom stop you from realizing your full economic potential?

Chapter 3: The Herd Effect

> *"If what you thought to be true turned out NOT to be, WHEN would you want to know about it?"*
> ~Don Blanton

Let's talk about everyday decision-making. You're hungry, and you find yourself in front of two restaurants. Both look good. Which one should get your business? You could hook up a laptop or visit the library computer, do a search for reviews, and see what people think of the two restaurants.

But like I said, you're hungry. *Really hungry!*

"Benign" herding behaviors may occur frequently in everyday decisions based on learning or observing information from others. Suppose that earlier, when both restaurants were empty, the first customer of the evening chose the restaurant on the left at random. Later, a couple looks in both windows. The restaurant on the right is empty. They move on to the restaurant on the right. And so on, with other customers making an assumption of quality based on the size of the crowd. "They must know something," you think as you join the herd. This sort of collective behavior is called an *information cascade*—joining in the behavior of others through observation, despite personal preferences or knowledge.

And information cascade isn't the only herd behavior we fall into:
- Anxiety
- Bandwagon effect
- Conventional wisdom
- Mob psychology
- Conformity

> *Once the herd starts moving in one direction, it's very hard to turn it, even slightly.*
> ~Dan Rather

Not that a decision like where to have dinner or what sports team to suddenly root for will affect the rest of your life. But what about choosing a financial vehicle? Do you really want to make a financial decision based on herd behavior? Birds and insects flock and swarm.

Smart individuals decide things objectively!

Chapter 4: The Parable of the Ham

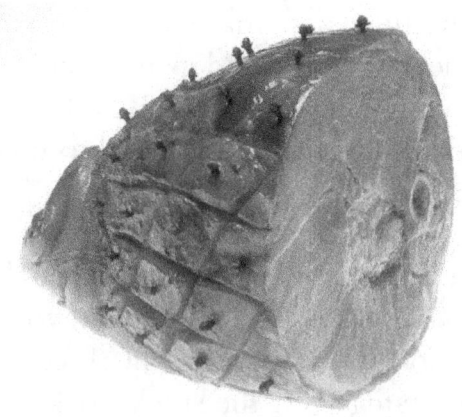

Sales guru Zig Ziglar tells a story that pertains to decision-making. He observed his wife cutting off the end of a ham before placing it into the oven to bake. He asked why. She explained that she'd always baked a ham that way, and that her mother had always done the same. Did he not like the ham?

Sure, he told her. He was simply curious. But the curiosity didn't go away, and when he met his mother-in-law later in the week, he asked her about the ham. Her answer was much the same as his wife's: "My mother always cut off the end of the ham before baking." His wife's mother's mother was a great cook. If something worked for her, then it had to be the right thing to do.

Curiosity unsated, he resolved to ask the family matriarch. Yes, the old woman admitted. The end of the ham had to come off before baking. It seems that when she'd first married, they didn't have much money for pots and pans. The one baking pan they owned was small, and most hams wouldn't fit. So she cut off the end to make it fit.

The chances are good that your parents had a passbook savings account. Does that mean you're going to let passbook savings be the focus of your investment strategy? Or the stock market? If you do, you may be cutting off more than just the end of the ham! Read on!

Chapter 5: Stress, Uncertainty and the Future

Another way people approach the decision-making process is to simply avoid making a decision. Before you laugh, take a look in the mirror and ask yourself if you've ever cancelled a doctor's or dentist's appointment.

The reason we avoid the doctor or dentist is often the same reason we avoid looking at our financial plans for the future. We subconsciously become comfortable with the uncertainty. But there are reasons for stepping out of our comfort zone. There is exhilaration in setting the goal, removing the uncertainty and seeing into the future.

And stress is a killer.

In nearly 20 years of reviewing clients insurance and retirement planning documents, we meet many people who want to avoid taking a detailed look at their current plan. It's easier to avoid looking. We have a natural aversion to address anything which may cause us pain. (I'm not talking about physical pain, but emotional anguish from the discovery that happy endings aren't automatic, and procrastination has a cost.)

> Luke 21:26
> *...men's hearts failing them from fear and the expectation of those things which are coming on the earth, for the heavens will be shaken.*

Financial fear and stress can actually result in depression. Signs include:
- Irritability (anger with no apparent reason, constant fighting)
- Feelings of being overwhelmed (confused by even simple decisions)
- Fatigue
- Loss of joy (in even simple pleasures)
- Feelings of guilt
- Sense of helplessness (or worthlessness)
- Lack of focus ('I don't know where to start, and if I do start, I can't seem to finish!)

In my personal journey, I remember discovering that the elements I thought were in place were actually missing. The realization was painful, and I did not want to admit I had procrastinated.

But there's reason for hope. Make the decision not to place blame, but to start from where you are *today*. Address the uncertainty in your life and begin to feel freedom.

Taking the time to complete a financial review can be difficult. The results can force us to look at things we wish to avoid. Visiting a doctor can bring a two-fold benefit (we no longer have to worry about maladies that don't apply, and if something *is* wrong, we can start treating it immediately). In the same way, honestly looking at your financial situation and preparing a plan for the future can bring new life and energy.

> Proverbs 21:5
> *The plans of the diligent lead to profit, as surely as haste leads to poverty.*

Uncertainty lends itself to fear and fear has a crippling effect on our future. Think of it this way: Suppose you are lost in a forest. Which way should you go? The answer to that question depends on *where you are now*. Finding out where you stand financially is the first step toward freedom from stress and uncertainty.

Removing uncertainty means freedom:
- Peace of mind
- Freedom from debt
- Freedom from worry over future tax burdens
- The ability to capitalize on opportunities

THE CA$H RESIDENCE

- The financial freedom afforded by a financial legacy

Which so much at stake, why not resolve to remove financial uncertainty from your life? Sound good? Read on!

> *When I was young I thought that money was the most important thing in life; now that I am old I know that it is.*
>
> ~Oscar Wilde

Part Two
Chapter 6: Three Types of People

Financial behaviors tend to fall into three big categories. Look at these three types, and ask yourself where you fit in. The answer might be enlightening:

The Spender
Lives paycheck to paycheck
Very little savings
Lives at the mercy of creditors
Has a JOB, but must pledge future earnings to buy high-ticket items

The Saver
Has savings and uses it to buy high-ticket items
Pays back savings, but loses the compound interest forever
May believe that being a saver will automatically guarantee a bright future

The CA$H Residence (PES)
CA$H bucket continues to be full and growing
Makes high-ticket purchases using OPM—other people's money

THE CA$H RESIDENCE

Cashes in on investment opportunities because the miracle of uninterrupted compound interest is…uninterrupted.

You probably don't recognize the term *CA$H Residence (PES)*. Don't worry, we'll discuss this term in depth before we're through. The *CA$H Residence* types recognize that the majority of Americans send 30-40 percent of their income to someone else's bank in the form of:
Mortgage interest
Credit Card payments
Student Loans
Car Payments

We will continue to have the need for finance throughout our lives. If we build our *CA$H Residence* for ourselves and our children and grandchildren, we create a "Legacy of Freedom" from the slavery to a system of financing.

Proverbs 22:7
The rich rule over the poor, and the borrower is slave to the lender.

The revolutionary idea that you could become your own banker owes much to R. Nelson Nash, the financial genius behind *Infinite Banking*. Instead of giving your money to another bank to use, why not finance major purchases with your own money, tax-free? Nash envisioned building a personal economic system, what I'm calling a CA$H Residence. And you can begin building your financial structure today. Read on, and find out more!

Chapter 7: Taxes – Up or Down?

> *In this world, nothing is certain but death and taxes.*
>
> ~Benjamin Franklin

The tax man cometh is a phrase which puts fear in the hearts of many. We all must pay taxes, and if you achieve any financial success, your share of the tax burden will be greater than others.

We always ask our clients, "What do you think? Are taxes going up or down?" In my experience, 100 percent of the people we asked think that taxes are going up. How could they think otherwise? All governments overspend. But what's disappointing is, taxes can go up with the single stroke of a pen and a new law. Without warning, lawmakers can change the rules and we are required to play by them.

With that kind of game, how can you win? Forget winning—how can you plan?

Based on current law, we do have some options to minimize the tax burden if we think ahead and implement a detailed plan. But when sorting possibilities, ask yourself, "Am I paying tax on the seed or the harvest?" Let me explain.

The Gospels share over 40 parables. In many of them, Jesus uses an understanding of agriculture—a common endeavor in that day—to deliver his message. Likewise, I would like to use an analogy using a farmer and his corn harvest to explain a problem with tax-deferred financial vehicles.

In the beginning of the season, the farmer prepares the ground, plants the seed and dreams of an abundant harvest. In some years, the harvest is plentiful. In other years, the farmer is disappointed. When a person decides to put a portion of their income into an IRA, they will get the tax deduction for the current year and pray for an abundant harvest at retirement.

But after due diligence, you may find that an IRA may not be the best choice. If the farmer had the option to pay the tax on the seed or pay the tax on the harvest, which would he choose? I submit that in most cases, he would choose to pay the tax on the seed. In both the Roth IRA and in the CA$H Residence system, we choose to pay the taxes on the seed.

There are three tax strategies for your retirement:
- Taxable

- Tax-deferred
- Tax-free.

These three strategies will have an impact on your taxes; either today's taxes or tomorrow's taxes!

Taxable - You pay tax now and invest with after-tax dollars. Then, you pay tax on all the earnings *as they are earned.* (Returning to our parable, this is like paying taxes on both the seed and on the harvest as it grows!) These investments are in non-qualified accounts such as savings accounts, CDs, stocks, and bonds.

Tax-deferred - You get a tax deduction now and invest with pre-tax dollars. You won't pay tax on the earnings until you use them. (This is like paying taxes on the whole harvest later.) These investments include your qualified accounts, such as a Traditional IRA and most pension plans. There are limits to how much you can contribute, and you are required to take the money out after the age of seventy and pay taxes. (But let's return to an earlier question—Will taxes be higher or lower in the future?)

Tax-free - You pay tax now (on the seed) and never pay taxes on the harvest. This is a ROTH IRA or the cash value in your life insurance. The ROTH IRA is limited to individuals under a certain income, whereas the life insurance contributions can be much higher.

But which path is best? That depends on the future of taxes. Tax rates answer to this question should determine your choice of financial vehicle. Let's look at some scenarios:

What if Tax Rates Stay the Same?

If tax rates stay the same, it doesn't matter if you pay tax now (on the seed) or later (on the harvest). The final outcome is the same, believe it or not:

Tax Rate Remains Constant (35%) 7% Growth for 20 years		Tax on Seed	Tax on Harvest	Gain/Loss
	Investment	100,000	100,000	
	After Tax	65,000		
	Future Value	251,570	387,030	
	Less Tax	0	<135,460>	
	Future Investment	$251,570	$251,570	$0

What if Tax Rates Go Down?

If tax rates go down, you would be better off paying tax on the harvest. In this scenario, you would save $27,100 by investing in your IRA or qualified accounts:

Tax Rate Decrease (35% to 28%) 7% Growth for 20 years		Tax on Seed	Tax on Harvest	Gain/ Loss
	Investment	100,000	100,000	
	After Tax	65,000		
	Future Value	251,570	387,030	
	Less Tax	0	<108,360>	
	Future Investment	$251,570	$278,670	$27,100

What if Tax Rates Go Up?

If tax rates go up, you would be better off paying tax on the seed. By investing in your ROTH IRA or your permanent life insurance policy, you could have saved $27,100.

Tax Rate Increase (35% to 42 %) 7% Growth for 20 years		Tax on Seed	Tax on Harvest	Gain/ Loss
	Investment	100,000	100,000	
	After Tax	65,000		
	Future Value	251,570	387,030	
	Less Tax	0	<162,560>	
	Future Investment	$251,570	$224,470	<$27,1000>

So what's the best path? Since we can't see the future, there's no certainty. We don't know where the tax rates will be in the future. We don't know who will be elected, and what legislation they will enact.

However, we do know that the government has hefty obligations. Social Security, Medicare and other programs must be funded. The country is, at the time of publication, $14 *trillion* in debt. Our government is already struggling to fund programs in today's dollars and our obligation may well grow exponentially.

The government's main source of income is taxation, and in order to fund these future obligations, additional funding could very well come from future tax increases.

What is the best course of action? Planning! In order to properly prepare for retirement and your taxes, having a plan that maximizes the potential for you to reach your goals, while minimizing taxes is best.

The examples in this chapter are hypothetical, and should not be taken as specific tax or investment advice. There are no guarantees in any investment return or tax rate. But having your assets placed in ways that minimize your taxes now and in the future will be critical as the tax rates change.

I'll ask you again: Do you think taxes will go up or down?

Chapter 8: The Perfect Asset?

As I said earlier, we will take an *objective* look at the most common financial vehicles in which we store our money. To list a few:
- Shoebox
- Certificate of Deposit (CD)
- Money Market Account
- 401K / IRA
- Home Equity loan
- Real Estate
- CA$H Residence/Private Economic System (PES)

You might find it funny that we listed a "shoebox" here. The other cliché you might have heard is "hiding your money in a mattress." Some people don't trust any investments at all. They figure that if they hold tight to their cash, they won't lose anything.

Are they right? No. Let me introduce another term: *opportunity costs*. Suppose you have a choice between working an extra shift at your job, and going to an amusement park. Going to the park will cost you $100. But that's not your only cost if you choose the amusement park. You pay to go to the park, and you lose the extra wages you might have earned. Opportunity costs are the loss of a potential gain from other choices when you settle on one alternative. In our example, if you settle on the amusement park, you pay to play, and you lose wages, too.

Look at the list of financial vehicles. Which ones carry hidden opportunity costs? (The answer may surprise you.) But let's compare some of the positive features of each type of investment here. I encourage you to objectively compare the benefits that each financial vehicle carries.

Shoebox
- Safety
- Liquidity
- Control

C.D. (Certificate of Deposit)
- Safety
- High contributions
- Collateral opportunities
- No- loss provision

Money Market Account
- Safety
- High contributions
- Collateral opportunities
- No- loss provision

Home Equity loan
- Tax-deferred growth
- Collateral opportunities

CA$H Residence (PES)
- Tax-deferred growth
- TAX-FREE distribution (Tax-Free Retirement)
- High contribution limits
- Collateral opportunities
- Safety—Principle that is NEVER at risk
- Guaranteed loan options
- Unstructured loan payments
- Liquidity—use and control
- Heirs receive inheritance TAX-FREE

By now, you're probably wondering what the CA$H Residence (PES) option entails. The benefits look good. But how does this option compare to, say, a 401K plan? Read on!

Chapter 9: 401k Chaos

Why wouldn't you want to put your money in a 401k plan? After all, conventional wisdom says that's the safest path to retirement.

> *To start off, I've never been a fan of the 401k...it's a real loser's bet if you think about it.*
> Daniel Ameduri

One thing's for sure: If you bank on a 401k, you won't be alone. The rest of the herd will be there with you. But let's take an objective look at the drawbacks to most 401k plans:

- Tax deferred plans can come back to bite you—taxes are likely to be *higher* when you retire.
- Many plans are booby-trapped (full of hidden fees that can eat away your growth.
- Lack of control.
- Limited investment options.
- The specter of inflation haunts most long-term plans.
- Promotes false security (allowing bad spending habits and an increased debt tolerance).

And think about this: you don't know what the future will bring. That means you can put your money into an IRA for thirty years and still not know how your financial future will end up. Do

THE CA$H RESIDENCE

you remember the stock crash of 2008? Can you imagine how people felt as they reached retirement age, only to read the bad news in the morning paper? And what about the opportunity costs of a traditional IRA?

Put another way, traditional IRAs join a list of investments that lock your money up in such a way that only financial institutions can use it. I call that idea, *money prison.*

Money prison? What a strange concept! But as we explore the various structures or vehicles we choose to put money in. we must always be aware of which vehicles give us access or restrict access to OUR money.

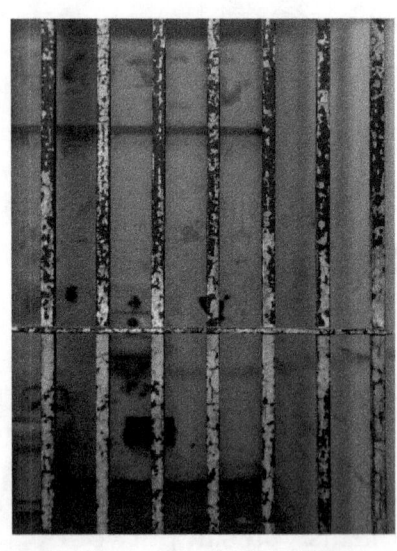

We know that cash gives us accessibility to our funds, but we give up opportunity costs. A savings or checking account gives us options and accessibility but again when we use it, we are transferring our funds to another bank. And we are giving up opportunity costs.

Real Estate can be a tremendous financial vehicle, but if our equity or cash is needed, we may have to sell the asset to use it.

While it's true that you can access the money (with some difficulty) from an IRA, the penalties and fees associated with using these funds are a huge drain on the future. IRAs are, in my opinion, money prisons. In return for tax *postponement,* you give up use of your own money.

Surely there's a better way to plan for the future while serving the present?

> *"Are you 100 percent sure you are going to have a great retirement, or do you have some doubts?"*
>
> Larry McLean, Your Family Bank

Part Three
Chapter 10: What Do Banks Know?

Suppose there was an institution that gathered the greatest minds in the financial world. Economists, accountants, financial analysts and attorneys, all under one roof, all focused on the efficient use of money. You'd want to know how they invested the institution's capital, wouldn't you? You'd want to know what the experts behind-the-scenes do to maximize growth and stability while reducing taxes.

I'm talking about banks.

If there's one institution that really understands the use of cash value life insurance, it's banks. These financial institutions are involved in most every aspect of our economy, and like many big corporations, banks appreciate the objective worth of this form of life insurance. What better way to fund employee healthcare, pensions and other benefits than with a safe, time-tested strategy?

So it's no surprise that banks are heavily invested in cash value life. Nearly every major bank makes their balance sheet public, according to FDIC rules and regulations. Take a look at just how much money some well-known banks hold in life insurance.

Banking Institution	Life Insurance Assets
Bank of America	$19,607,000,000
Wells Fargo Bank	$17,739,000,000
J.P. Morgan Chase Bank	$10,327,000,000
U. S. Bank	$5,451,892,000

Banks place billions of dollars into life insurance. Is that important? You bet it is. Banks are in the money business. Placing their money in cash value life insurance is so common, financial experts have coined jargon to describe it, including "bank-owned life insurance" (BOLI). When corporations do the same, it's called "corporate-owned life insurance" (COLI).

The FDIC allows Life Insurance Assets to be classified as *Tier 1* capital—the safest capital. The amount of Tier 1 capital a bank has is considered to be a good measure of the bank's financial strength and stability.

As mentioned, corporations are following the cash value life insurance strategy as a means of providing predictable income while minimizing risk. The companies in the list below all hold life insurance as an asset:

☐ General Electric

THE CA$H RESIDENCE

- ☐ Walt Disney
- ☐ Proctor & Gamble
- ☐ Crown Holdings
- ☐ AT&T
- ☐ Amway
- ☐ Nestle
- ☐ Panera Bread
- ☐ Prudential Insurance
- ☐ NetLife
- ☐ General Motors
- ☐ Harley Davidson
- ☐ H.J. Heinz
- ☐ International Paper
- ☐ Johnson & Johnson
- ☐ Lockheed Martin
- ☐ Lucent Technologies
- ☐ McGraw-Hill
- ☐ Norfolk Southern
- ☐ Outback Steak House
- ☐ Pfizer
- ☐ Pacific Gas & Electric
- ☐ Gannett Publishing
- ☐ Dow Chemical
- ☐ Lillian Vernon
- ☐ Bed, Bath and Beyond
- ☐ Cendant
- ☐ CSX
- ☐ Monsanto
- ☐ BellSouth
- ☐ Office Depot
- ☐ Nike
- ☐ Starbucks

David Saucer

- ☐ United Healthcare
- ☐ Ryder Systems
- ☐ Anheuser-Busch
- ☐ Newell Rubbermaid
- ☐ KB Home
- ☐ Avon
- ☐ CVS
- ☐ Comcast
- ☐ United Technologies

Chapter 11: The Phenomenon of Uninterrupted Compound Interest

Cash value life insurance? It's been around for centuries. Edmund Halley, the astronomer who discovered Halley's Comet, also developed the first actuarial table. His work was continued by James Dodson, the 18th century mathematician, leading to the first life insurance company, founded in London.

In the Americas, the first life insurance ventures were spearheaded by Presbyterian and Episcopalian churches. When the massacre of George Armstrong Custer at the Battle of the Little Bighorn stranded a number of families in the West, public sentiment for the protection afforded by life insurance gave birth to a vibrant new industry.

Cash value life insurance—your CA$H Residence (PES) solution, is a type of life insurance that pays out when the policyholder dies, but it also accumulates cash value during the policyholder's lifetime. What makes it work?

I've referred to *compound interest* as the '8th Wonder of the World," but interest loses its wonder and amazement when it is interrupted. Mathematically speaking, the formula below expresses compound interest if P is the original principle and X is the rate of interest expressed as a decimal. At the end of the nth year, the compounded amount will be:

$$P(1 + X)n$$

Confused? Understand this: the growth of the compound amount—the total value of your investment—is exponential, not linear. That only works, if you have uninterrupted compounding.

To understand exponential growth, let's review an old riddle: *Would you rather I give you $1,000,000 dollars or a Penny a day doubled for 31 days?*

> Proverbs 13:11
>
> *Dishonest money dwindles away, but whoever gathers money little by little makes it grow.*

A million dollars would be great, but if I understand the phenomenon of uninterrupted compounding and exponential growth, I would make a different choice.

THE CA$H RESIDENCE

Doubling a Penny for 30 Days	
Day 1 $.01	Day 16 $327.68
Day 2 $.02	Day 17 $655.36
Day 3 $.04	Day 18 $1,310.72
Day 4 $.08	Day 19 $2,621.44
Day 5 $.16	Day 20 $5,242.88
Day 6 $.32	Day 21 $10,485.76
Day 7 $.64	Day 22 $20,971.52
Day 8 $1.28	Day 23 $41,943.04
Day 9 $2.56	Day 24 $83,886.08
Day 10 $5.12	Day 25 $167,772.16
Day 11 $10.24	Day 26 $335,544.32
Day 12 $20.48	Day 27 $671,088.64
Day 13 $40.96	Day 28 $1,342,177.28
Day 14 $81.92	Day 29 $2,684,354.56
Day 15 $163.84	Day 30 $5,368,709.12

So which is it? $1,000,000 or $ 5,368,709?

Perhaps you recall the Biblical parable of the *talents.* A wealthy man entrusted a number of talents (a monetary unit worth 20 years in wages) to his servants. One servant received five talents, another two, and a third servant received one talent. When the man returned from his journeys, he asked each servant what they'd done with the money he'd left with them. The servant who'd shepherded five talents had invested them, and doubled his talents—he now had ten. The servant who had two talents had doubled his as well—he now had four talents. The servant who had one talent had taken it and buried it in the ground, untouched. He still had the one talent, intact, but he'd done nothing to increase the wealth.

The wealthy man then did something unusual. He took the single talent and gave it to the servant who already had ten, admonishing, "Thou wicked and slothful servant!" The lessons are clear. Even the Bible worries over opportunity costs! And though we all start with different circumstances, and all end up with different results, *it's what we do with what we have that matters.*

Scripture is clear on the subject of wealth. Riches are a gift from God, to be used in His service. We are stewards, encouraged to increase the blessing through investment and directed toward generosity to others.

Continuous compounding is a wealth creation strategy that allows you to be a wise steward of the gifts in your life. So, are you going to bury your money in the ground, or put it where it can do the most good?

Chapter 12: Famous Examples of CA$H Residence or PES Phenomenon

When taking an *objective* look at investment options, one important thing to do is to look back for a track record of how a particular option worked out for people in the past. Let's take a look back at some famous, respected entrepreneurs and the companies they founded, and see what the role of cash value life insurance played in their success.

Nearly Wiped Out

The stock market crash of 1929 destroyed a lot of companies. One chain of dry goods stores, supplying important goods to mining and farm families, was particularly hard hit. The owner suffered from the effects of great physical and mental strain. And his company was nearly wiped out.

What saved John Cash Penney was his cash value life insurance policies. At a time of desperate need, he was able to borrow against those policies to pay his employees and keep his company running. After the Great Depression, the company—J.C. Penney—was able to rebound and become one of the greatest retail companies in the country. Today, the company boasts more than 1,100 stores worldwide, doing $18 billion a year in sales.

An Icon is Born

Ray was one of three partners who dreamed of creating a hamburger empire. The other two partners sold out after six years, though the chain still bears their name. Meanwhile, Ray built the company despite almost constant cash-flow problems.

Anyone who knows about rapid business growth knows that sometimes, companies grow *too* fast. The bills can pile up quicker than the revenues, and suddenly, the success story is over. Ray was smart, though, and for the first eight years, he didn't even take a salary. When times were tough, he helped cover the salaries of key employees by borrowing against his cash value life insurance policies.

Ray Kroc believed in the power of advertising. Though it's not well known, Ray also used his cash value life insurance to help finance a marketing campaign featuring a clown that would become a fixture in American pop culture—Ronald McDonald. The rest is history.

Today, McDonalds serves more than 50 million people a day at more than 30,000 locations across the globe.

A Clean Amusement Park

Back in the day, amusement parks were pretty shady places. Carneys ran run-down attractions, rip-off "games of skill" and dangerous rides. Walter had a vision for a family-friendly amusement park that catered to the hopes and dreams of children. Needless to say, investors didn't fall over themselves to give Walter—a cartoonist turned entrepreneur—the money he needed.

The vision was unique. Walter told a friend, "I want it to look like nothing else in the world. And it should be surrounded by a train." After five years of planning, the project was launched. What many people don't know is, Walt Disney helped finance

Disneyland and other projects with cash value life insurance policies.

Think of what an impact Disneyland has had on our culture! Our whole perception of amusement parks has changed, thanks to the vision of the man who gave us feature-length cartoons, television shows and, of course, a certain mouse...

From Typhoid to Tutelage

Leland and Jane lost a son to typhoid fever, a devastating disease that plagued mankind for centuries (typhoid once wiped out a third of the population in ancient Athens, Greece). To compensate for the loss of their son, the couple decided to dedicate their lives to helping other people's children. They founded a University, and enrolled 555 students in just the first year.

Then, tragedy struck again. Leland died just two years after the university's founding, leaving Jane with financial struggles and the prospect of a failed enterprise.

But Jane would not give up on the dream. She was able to survive six years of fragile finances with the proceeds from her husband's cash value life insurance. The faculty was paid and operations continued uninterrupted.

Today, Stanford University, Leland and Jane Stanford's dream, boasts more than 15,000 students, both graduate and undergraduate. The university is one of the most respected schools in the country.

What's Cooking?

Doris had been a Tupperware salesperson, and was actually pretty successful at it. The business model seemed sound. But wouldn't she be even more successful running a company of her own, using a similar model?

Doris believed that some of the cooking tools available to women in the home were inferior to the ones available to chefs in restaurants. She imagined success selling professional-quality cooking products in-home, using the "sales party" techniques she'd learned. Using her cash value life insurance policy, Doris funded a company that started in her basement and became a national phenomenon.

Today, Pampered Chef is a billion-dollar enterprise with more than 12 million customers. Doris Christopher turned a dream and a vision into a fortune.

But not without financial help.

Financial help that is available to you. Is cash value life insurance a good option for your personal economic system (PES)? Read on.

Chapter 13: Public Company vs. Mutual Company

Not all cash value life insurance is equal. One difference involves the company you purchase the policy from. What's the difference between a public company and a mutual company?

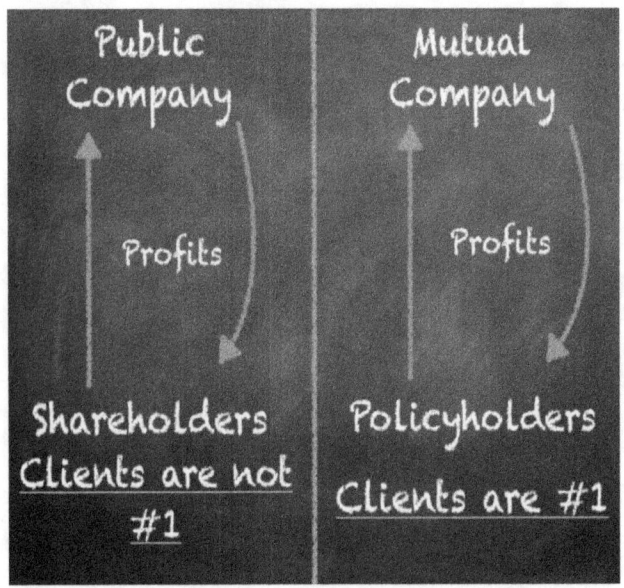

Simple answer: A mutual company is owned by the policy holders. A public company is owned by shareholders and pleasing the shareholders is the primary goal.

A mutual company is a company with a specific objective, owned by policyholders who receive dividends and capital gains according to predetermined formula. The policy holders (clients) are first in line to share in the profits of the company *because they own the company*.

A stock company is owned by shareholders. The stock company has a specific mission to create profit for its shareholders. Clients are a means, not an end.

The stock company is under no obligation to return dividends to shareholders and shareholders will only receive capital gains if the sale of the shareholders ownership has greater value than the purchase price. Management's objective in a stock company is to provide shareholder value through appreciation of the shares of stock.

The mutual company's shares might also appreciate in value if the underlying investments increase in value, which would result in a higher portfolio worth (and thus higher net asset value per share).

Given the choice, I would *always* recommend a Mutual company, which pays dividends back to the policy owners.

Chapter 14: CA$H Residence—a Personalized Economic System

Let's recap. Cash value life insurance is a vehicle to help you create a CA$H Residence. This is a personalized economic system with a stunning array of benefits, including:

- Tax-Deferred growth
- TAX-FREE Distribution (Tax-Free Retirement)
- Competitive returns
- High Contribution limits
- Collateral Opportunities
- Principle that is NEVER at Risk
- Interest that is Guaranteed
- Guaranteed Loan options
- Unstructured Loan payments
- Liquidity, Use and Control
- Safety
- Heirs receive inheritance Tax- Free

One aspect of the CA$H Residence strategy that we've not yet discussed is the possibility for building *generational wealth*. We're all familiar with generational poverty, so difficult for the modern family to escape. But instead of a vicious cycle of poverty and meager entitlements, what if we were empowered to not only better our circumstances, but start a pattern of wealth-building that continued on to our children and our children's children? That's what using a tax-free distribution is all about!

No uncertainty. No stress. Your future assured. What's the downside? You'll have to do a little research. Study the various financial vehicles *objectively*. Decide what options are important to *you*. And if you opt for the CA$H Residence option, you'll have to show a little courage and break free from the herd.

Chapter 15: CA$H Residence for Business

The CA$H Residence (PES) process will change the present and the future for individuals, but it can also make a dramatic impact on a Business.

The same principles that apply to individuals are in play for business, and because a business is always in search of the most advantageous and strategic use of capital, the CA$H Residence system can increase a business's profitability in a tremendous way.

Every business faces the same variables, whether it is a doctor's office or a construction company:
- Expenses
- Lease or rent
- Equipment
- Health insurance
- Fuel
- Utilities

Using a *cost recovery* strategy, you can:
- Recover part or all of the monies spent on targeted expenses while recording them as an expense to the business
- Recover the lost opportunity cost
- Use the CA$H Residence model to become your own source of financing.

David Saucer

- Supplement and create a Tax- Free Retirement

Chapter 16: Case Studies

April Jones took a job in a dental office as a receptionist. As time passed, she took on more tasks at the office, including scheduling and light bookkeeping. Over time, she became invaluable to the office, and in turn, she began to think of her job as a career. With that realization, April decides to plan her future.

She fills out a personal financial plan and, after evaluating options that fit her income, opts for a cash value life insurance policy.

April isn't rich, but she has no intention of being poor. Paying a premium of $250 a month, she will invest a total of $105,000 between her present age (32) and her projected retirement age (67). Her payout after retirement, spread over 20 years, will be $371,185!

Ken Harmon is a business owner. His restaurant struggled for the first year, then took off. Now, at age 37, he finds himself with the "hot" restaurant in the area. Ken wants to plan for the future. Restaurant work involves long, hard hours. When he retires, Ken wants to enjoy his family and his free time.

Because he's successful, Ken can afford a cash value policy with a big monthly premium. He pays $2,500 every month. If he retires at 67—30 years later—what will he have paid in? What will his policy be worth?

Ken will have invested $900,000 in his CA$H Residence. At the end of 30 years, that investment will yield a 20-year annuity, with an annual payout of $122,999; a total of $3,817,900 (tax free). Chances are, Ken will be able to do a lot of dining out during his retirement. Big tipper? For sure.

Pat Cabrerra is a medical doctor. At the age of 40, she's seen a lot of patients reach their later years with limited means and failing health. That's not going to happen to her! After researching all of the possibilities, Pat decides to buy a cash value life insurance policy. She plans to retire at 65. What will her choice mean to her in terms of dollars?

Pat pays a $1,000 per month premium. Over 25 years, that means an investment of $300,000. (Of course, she has access to tax-free loans from her policy, which she takes advantage of twice when medical advances mean new equipment purchases.)

When Pat retires, her death benefit has a value of $712,952. But Pat's alive and well, enjoying an annual payout of $59,720 for the next 25 years.

That's more than enough to allow her to concentrate on volunteer medical work in South America—a dream she's planned to fulfil since her days as an intern.

> *My interest is in the future because I am going to spend the rest of my life there.*
> ~Charles Kettering

Epilogue

The journey to freedom is a path many look for and never find. Freedom from the shackles of normalcy and mediocrity. Freedom from fear and uncertainty. Freedom from the herd.

Life is about launching into the unknown and breaking free. This relentless pursuit is seen in the drive and actions of entrepreneurs and dreamers. Think back to the early history of this country. Can you imagine the drive of the men and women who left everything and headed west? Sometimes without maps, without guides. They packed their belongings in wagons, taking only what was necessary, and forged ahead in search of a dream. And their friends and family? Most stayed behind.

> *Be sure you're right, then go ahead.*
> ~David Crockett, Frontiersman

SWSWSW is an acronym I frequently use in training and workshops. The acronym is an attitude and mindset which must be adopted.

Some Will, Some Won't, So What?

THE CA$H RESIDENCE

I challenge you to break free and release the weights that bind your mind.

I implore you to choose the "road not taken."

About the Author

David is a lifelong resident of Louisiana. In the second year of seminary, he saw a girl in the lunch line and his life was changed—he's been happily married for more than 25 years.

David has two children. Kaleb is 22 and Chloe' is 20. His children are his greatest joy, and he proudly proclaims his greatest calling is to be a Dad.

As a licensed minister, he has joyfully served in many capacities. Over two decades, he has been involved in the financial services industry, helping thousands of families and business strategically plan for the future.

David's passion is family and making lasting memories.

Appendix A: Life Insurance—an Overview

The CA$H Residence (PES) approach to building wealth specifies cash value life insurance. But there's more than one kind of life insurance. What are the different types, and how do they differ?

Term Life Insurance pays a benefit to survivors in the event of the death of an insured person. Policies are in force for a set period of time. When the policy expires, it's up to the insured party to purchase another policy. Term life has no investment component.

Whole Life Insurance combines a death benefit with an investment component. The cash value of the policy builds, tax-deferred, until the policy matures. You can borrow money against that accumulation, tax-free. Whole life is a *cash value life insurance,* as described in this book.

Universal Life Insurance combines a death benefit with a money-market type investment for a higher rate of return. Unlike cash value (whole life), the higher rate of return cannot be guaranteed because it's tied to stocks and bonds that involve risk.

Appendix B: A Personal Plan for Financial Success

In my work for the financial industry, I've found that most people have already done some financial planning. Maybe they have some investments and some insurance. Perhaps they have employee benefits, or even a will. What they don't have is an understanding of how all of the pieces fit together.

A properly trained financial strategist will work on what they call the offensive and defensive sides of planning. The offensive side consists of savings, wealth accumulation and entrepreneurial ventures. The defensive side involves protecting against risk. The CA$H Residence attends to both the offensive and defensive.

Another aspect to consider involves the evolution of thinking. Simply put, you don't think the same way when you're 80 years old as when you're 25. We consistently hear older clients ask, "Why didn't someone explain this to me when I was younger?"

For these reasons, it's imperative that you really understand and comprehend the possibilities.

THE CA$H RESIDENCE

Now that you've read the book, you might have questions. Can I do this? Where do I begin?

Yes, you can build a financial future. Doing so involves beginning a journey of learning. There are possibilities and benefits to weigh. The subject of money is layered with nuance. I learn something new and exciting nearly every day. By reading this book, you've taken the first step on your own journey.

Knowing where you want to go is part of the formula. You need to set goals. But you also need to know where you are right now. Suppose you wanted to travel to Chicago. Would you go west? East? *Your direction depends on your starting point.*

So, ask yourself: Where am I now? What have I done so far? Answering those questions involves gathering some information:

Certificates of Deposit	$ _____
IRA/401K	$ _____
Cash Savings	$ _____
CASH value Life insurance	$ _____
Desired age for retirement	_____
Age _____ Spouse's Age	_____

Children's Ages   _____

Then, do your homework. Take an *objective* look at your options. If you happen to want more information from me, you are welcome to call for an appointment or e-mail me. I would be honored to help you with your personalized plan.

Contact Information:

David Saucer
Managing Director of Southern Region
Strategy. Opportunity. Integration.

Direct Line – 225.907.6000
Fax – 225.590.5596

www.CALLC.US
David.Saucer@CALLC.US

Baton Rouge | Little Rock
Los Angeles | Monroe | Nashville

Appendix C: Suggested Reading

Now that you've begun your learning journey, here is some suggested reading to help you on your way:

- Becoming Your Own Banker (Nelson Nash)
- Financial Independence in the 21st Century (Dwayne Burnell, MBA)
- The Great Wall Street Retirement Scam (Rick Bueter)
- How Privatized Banking Really Works (L. Carlos Lara and Robert P. Murphy, Ph.D.)
- The Millionaire Next Door (Thomas Stanley and William Danko)
- Opportunity Cost in Finance and Accounting (H. G. Heymann and Robert Bloom)
- The Richest Man in Babylon (George S. Clayson)
- The Trillion Dollar Meltdown (Charles R. Morris)
- Understanding the Modern Culture Wars (Paul A. Cleveland, Ph.D.)

Citations

"Brainy Quote" n.d. Web 22 Sep 2014.
http://www.brainyquote.com/

"Doubling Pennies" n.d. Web 22 Sep 2014.
http://mathforum.org/dr.math/faq/faq.doubling.pennies.html

"FDIC: Institution Directory." *FDIC: Institution Directory*. N.p., n.d. Web. 31 Dec. 2013

"RMS Manual of Examination Policies." *Federal Deposit Insurance Corporation*, n.d. Web. 2 Jan. 2014.
<http://www.fdic.gov/regulations/safety/manual/section3-7.pdf>.

"Things People Said: Bad Predictions" n.d. Web 22 Sep 2014.
http://www.rinkworks.com/said/predictions.shtml

www.ingramcontent.com/pod-product-compliance
Lightning Source LLC
Chambersburg PA
CBHW071800170526
45167CB00003B/1105